Lie To This is my story.

Rodney E. Corley

Editor: Dr. Yasmine Johnson

Published in Nashville, Tennessee *by BN Publications LLC*

Copyright © 2023 Rodney Corley

All rights reserved.

ISBN: **9798867969233**

This book is a memoir. It reflects the author's present recollections of experiences over time. This book is a book of memory, and memory has its own story to tell. I have done my best to tell a truthful story. The truth from memories and reflections.

DEDICATION

In loving memory of my great-grandfather, Overy Corley, and grandmother, Violet Rose Corley.

Uncle Charles Hawkins and Uncle Harry (Bally Jones) Corley. Auntie Cynthia Robinson Corley, Auntie Cheryl Rose Corley Sawyers, and Uncle Jimmy Glenn Corley Sawyers aka WC. Big Brother Edmund Deon Corley aka Fudd, Cousin Sabrina Hope Corley, and Cousin Alfonzo Corley. Hoppa, I never knew your real name, but I knew your love.

A Special Dedication to Auntie Mary Ann Corley aka May'ran RIP

I am Rodney and this is my story.

CONTENTS

DEDICATION iii

CONTENTS v

Acknowledgements vi

Give Me Game 1

SHit Real 3

Lil Tommy 4

Back to my Shit 5

Nine 7

UNCLE Tick 10

South Eighth 11

Speak Truth 13

MOMMY I'm Back 14

Welcome home gran-daddy 17

PATRICK Greer Aka Pat 19

CANDY GIRL 23

ACKNOWLEDGEMENTS

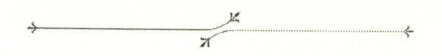

To all my niggaz on lock-down. I know you are fed up, but you gotta keep ya head up. I spent thirty plus years altogether in prison, so I know the feeling.

Special shoutout to my nigga Mac Man,
you know you my muthafuckin' REAL NIGGA! LUV FOOL!

My Lil Man MikAnthony. Luv ya, Lil Man.

To all my relatives: Uncle Tick, Auntie Jackie, Cuzo,
you all know who you are!

Last but not least, My OG- AEC.

It is mind over muthafuckin matter. If you don't mind it doesn't muthafuckin matter. Because those that matter don't mind and those that mind don't muthafuckin matter!

GIVE ME GAME

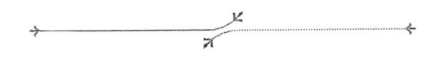

It was an early Saturday morning, the day that I was introduced to the most valuable knowledge of my life: the game of hustle, playing cards and shooting dice. The year was around 1972 and I was six years old. My family lived in the housing projects, University Court, located on the southside of Nashville, Tennessee. My Auntie MaryAnn Corley, we called her May'ran, lived with us. She was our live-in nanny. Auntie also had an ole' man named Hoppa, who lived with us as well. He was something extra special to me. He is the one that gave me the game on the hustle of playing cards and shooting dice. He was the first man to make me feel special. I mean really, special. He really took to me. May'ran, had everything to do with that because of how she took to me too. For what reason at the time I didn't know, but my closeness to her, for my whole life, says a lot.

I was the baby of five boys at the time. While all my older brothers were outside playing in the dirt, I was on grown folks' shit, being responsible and shit. I was under May'ran as her sidekick, her right-hand man. Learning how to cook, wash dishes, clean up the house and shit. She worked my ass now that I'm thinking about it! She always knew she could depend on me and believe me. Depending on me she did because she knew what she had instilled in me.

As I said, May'ran was our nanny. Ya,' nigga I was privileged. Ya', I grew up in the projects with a muthafuckin' nanny. She took care of us and the household because our mother worked two jobs. My mother did that shit all her life, worked, worked, and worked. And provide for us she did. My mother paid the bills and May'ran did the raising. Thank you, Auntie! (RIP BABY.) I remember too, growing up Uncle Bally (Bally Jones), Auntie Elaine (Uncle Bally's wife), and Auntie Cherly (Cher'rose) coming over to the house. Elaine and Cherly were May'ran's partners. They would be playing happy music, drinking, smoking, and playing Pokeno for money, a board game that you played with cards.

May'ran would run everyone out of the house, but me. My big brothers were happy to go outside to play in the dirt. I couldn't do that shit. I would stay on the high porch and just watch their asses. She would look out the door or window and see me on the high porch. She would ask me, "why aren't you outside playing?" I would respond, "I don't wanna play in no dirt." "I don't blame you," she would continue, "well, you can come in here and help me some so I can enjoy myself a little." And that's how Auntie and I were always on the same page. She knew she could trust and depend on me.

University Court was a living nightmare. I was too young to understand that the projects were designed to destroy the black family structure. I saw way too much violence. I remember at about 7 or 8 years old we would hear gunshots and run from it; but then after a while, you start to run to it. Violence starts to become a part of you. I started to embrace it as a natural part of my life which caused me to no longer fear violence. It was around that same time that I started going through the "wishing I had my father shit." This nigga, John Arthur French (Peewee) was staying in the same projects as I, but he was living with a whole other family. Not one of the six kids in that house belonged to him. He was doing shit for them and didn't do shit for me or my two brothers, James, and Jr. RIP Pops. That was some painful shit for me. I started to act out and become a problem child.

SHIT REAL

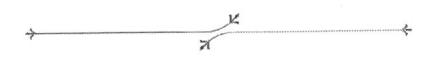

We didn't have many positive things to do during those times. I remember when throwing rocks at each other was a part of our recreation. We were serious about mastering rock throwing. I loved the curved rocks. Those were the rocks that would go in a curve and hit yo ass after you ran behind a building.

My dad had me so deep in my feelings one day, that I hit his ass with a nice size rock. He talked shit about how I bet not hit him with the rock while he took down a part of a branch off a tree, and said he was going to whip my ass if I hit him with the rock. I didn't care about shit he was saying. I was hurting inside for his love, time, and attention that I wasn't getting. My heart wanted him to feel my hurt. I said, "fuck you" and hit his ass with that rock and took off running. He didn't even try to catch me. I would have gladly taken that ass whipping just to have some of his attention for a few minutes. But I wasn't even worth an ass whipping to him. I went on playing with my only friend Lil Tommy. We were always together. I knew he and I were family in some kind of way, but I just didn't know how at the time.

It was early in the afternoon when that shit with my dad happened. Lil Tommy and I had run around the projects doing nothing all day before Tommy's mother, Ms. May Frances, called him to go into the house. Ms. Frances always made Tommy go in early. I would still be outside with the other "bad ass kids" whose parents was busy drinking, having fun, and not caring about what the kids do.

LIL TOMMY

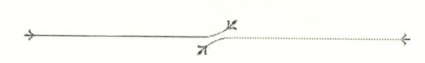

Lil Tommy was my first best friend. We go back 50 years. It would take Lil Tommy to really tell you just how bad I was as a child. Even till this day when the subject comes up Lil Tommy says, "Man, yo ass was bad as hell." He took too many ass whippings because of me. He reminds me of how I would grab grown women by their ass, rub their pussy, lift their dress and run. How I would curse out anybody, even the police, hit the older kids with sticks, bats, and bricks. How I carried a knife sometimes and tried to cut a few of the older, bigger dudes. He, lil Tommy, was there for me throughout the 28 ½ years I did straight in jail. Always making the time to talk, to drop off some ends for me or whatever (you know what I mean by whatever). Lil Tommy is a friend like no other I've ever had. We have always been close, genuine love and mutual respect. Neither one of us has ever hurt each other. We have man to man conversations, where we turn to each other to find the answer(s) to understanding how to truly love a woman properly. We both acknowledge that it is in our nature to love and provide for our family. We take pride in having that law as a universal law, nature of a man. We don't lie, sugar coat or make excuses for each other. I have that quality of relationship with all my niggaz. We don't bullshit each other. We don't have to agree to stay all right with each other, but we always have to be real about shit to remain true to each other. I can't fake and pretend that a nigga is right on some shit he wrong about to pacify his ego, real is real. That's the foundation Lil Tommy and I stand on.

Love you, Bruh. Appreciate cha always.

BACK TO MY SHIT

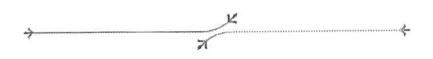

It was crazy in the hood. Everybody would be out all through the projects. That's a part of the excitement of being in the hood, you always had something to get into. The fast girls would be out at night with us. We would go into empty buildings and hunch. That was the shit to us during those times. If you got to grind on a girl, you were doing something. I had this girl named Linda. She and I were crazy about each other. We both were fast as hell. She let me touch her naked pussy. We never had real sex, just kid sex. Growing up in the projects was fun and crazy at the same damn time. The hoes. The drugs. The violence. The hood. A place where you learned about life the hard way and loved it. We didn't know anything different.

I mentioned earlier that we threw rocks at each other for recreation. Soon the rocks turned to bricks and at some point. All of us were throwing bricks at each other and got our heads busted. And that shit started family fights. Fights that ended up with families killing each other for years. Muthafucka's are still enemies till this day. Families that have hated each other for 50 years, all started from kids throwing rocks. Shit crazy!

It was a few weeks later when I was running through the projects on my way up to the U, where my dad stayed with that "bitch," as I use to call her under my breath. I was looking for my dad when lil Tommy ran up to me, breathing hard saying, "come on man, dude stabbing Peewee." I ran with him up to the U and sure-as-shit stinks dude was on top of my dad stabbing him. He was talking shit to my dad as he was taking his time stabbing him. I tried grabbing the man's arm, but he just pushed me down. My dad was trying to fight him off some, but he was too damn drunk to do much. I grabbed my most dangerous weapon, at the time. Yeah, you guessed it right, a brick, and knocked that nigga ass out with it. I grabbed my dad up with lil Tommy's help and took him over the bridge to Nashville General Hospital. My dad ended up with nine stab wounds to his head and neck and almost bled to death. I saved his life. The people at the hospital said told him I did, in front of me. They said, "You need to really be thankful for your son, because he saved your life." If we waited for an ambulance he would have surely died.

Still, that shit didn't change nothing and that was the early part of '73. Things were changing, again. My dad had kinda faded away and went back to prison again. During that time Hoppa was there and he made me feel what it felt like to have love from a dad. He embraced me and showed me nothing but love. He is the one that taught me the game of hustle, playing cards, and shooting dice. They both have always been an asset in my life. As I said, my real father was never around much. I didn't know that all those times when my dad wasn't around, he was running from the police and drunk as hell.

My mother never said anything negative about my dad during the times when he was in prison, which was most of my childhood life. Moms took us to visit almost every weekend. He would promise so many things, while in prison. Only to do nothing once he was out. Hoppa, was in my life. I started not wanting to go see him because Hoppa gave me attention and I liked Hoppa. He took me to the store and put me on his shoulders. That always made me smile and feel happy. I am smiling as I write this because of the memories. It's been about 48 years ago. Yet, my heart still remembers the joy and happiness he made me feel through the love he always gave to me.

One day Hoppa said he had to leave. He told me he was going to be leaving and he didn't know if he would be able to come back. I asked him, "why he wasn't coming back?" He said, "I am sick." I didn't understand that it meant that he was dying. He left that day and I never saw him again. Yet, he has always remained with me, all throughout my life. Another one of my Angels.

RIP Hoppa Love ya, lots!

NINE

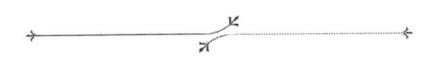

Hoppa was around until I was about 8 years old. Since he had taught me the game of Hussle, I taught all the young niggas how to play dice. We only shot for pennies, but that was a lot during those days. You could get a lot of cookies and shit for five cents. We also had the hobby shop, right across the street from Howard school. That's where we would go to play basketball and board games like pool and air hockey. Going to the hobby shop was an escape from the hood for me. In the hood we played hide and seek, catch, and go get it. That was the game I liked the most, catch the girl you like and go get it. Just a little kiss, but that was big for our age. During that time, school was fun for me. I was going to Cameron School where all the teachers were Black like me. They made school fun for us, but I fought a lot. My family had taught me that if my brothers were in a fight, we all fight, no matter what or who. I was supposed to fight with my brothers.

In 1975, I was 9 years old and that is when my life of crime started. I caught my first charge for assault against a police officer. We were at the Howard School swimming pool being destructive and committing acts of vandalism. The police came and grabbed my brother, Jr. told the police, "Let my brother go!" I kicked the police and took off running. The police pulled his gun out and said, "Stop nigga, before I kill yo' nigga ass." My brother Jr. and cousin Sabrina were begging for me to stop. They were crying, screaming and shit. So, I stopped. The police made me walk back to him. Once I was close enough, he grabbed me and slammed me on my face on the ground, in the grass. That shit hurt. I hit the ground hard as hell, face down, shit knocked the breath out of my ass. I couldn't even catch my breath to holla for my momma. He snatched my ass up off the ground and walked me to juvey (kid jail). Just a few steps and I was in juvey.

That was my first time in, and I didn't like that shit. They took your belt, and made you leave your shoes outside the door. It was a big ass slab made of concrete, designed to be a part of your bed. The thin ass mat they gave you was too damn thin. You could feel the concrete all through your body when you laid on that muthafucka. I made a lying ass promise to myself that day; that I ain't never coming back ever again. My mother was forced to come and get me after being there for a few hours. I was happy as hell to see her. The ass-whipping I had coming wasn't even on my mind. She was really upset when she came and got me. She had tears in her eyes. I didn't even understand why she was crying. Once outside, she grabbed me and held me tight. She told me that I was lucky the police didn't kill me for kicking him. I still didn't really understand why she was crying. I knew nothing about the Civil Rights Movement, police brutality, or the unlawful killings of blacks by white police officers. I knew nothing of the nightmare that we lived as black people in white America. I was just a kid! No one explained that shit to me. I didn't see black and white, it was all black to me, and it was love in the hood.

The pimps, players, hoes, hustlers, drug dealers, robbers, and thieves looked out for the kids. They ALL looked out for us. You had No Neck, Bug Head, Dead Eye, Catfish, Jump Sharp, and Lil Charles. But the one I looked up to the most and who used to really take personal time with me was Lonnie Hayes, he was a real killa. A pretty boy as some would say, but he was cool yet crazy. As the niggaz in the hood would say.

A lot of niggaz in the hood just avoided his ass, as best as they could. Females' pussy would get wet for him out of fear and desire. He was a gangstas', gangsta. Yeah, that type of gangsta but I never felt scared of him. He was like a big brother to me. He would always give me a few minutes of some game. He would say shit like," you can't be no punk, we got to show these niggaz and bitches that we ain't nothing to play with." He was killed by the police. They shot him down in cold blood.

Violet Rose Corley RIP Gran-Mommy'
We all love and miss ya.
RIP Queen
Love Ya'

A month or so after that I went to stay with my grandmother, Ms. Violet Rose Corley. My grandmother was everybody's mother and grandmother. She loved people, period. She would feed the whole neighborhood with the last of the food in the house. She lived at 853 South Eighth Street, at the time. I was enrolled in Warren School at the time where my cousin Sabrina Corley went too. For some reason, the cross-track girls from Settle Court and The Bottom couldn't stand Sabrina. Every day after school there was someone fighting for their life. Them bitches always wanted to gang my cousin. I don't know why but one thing fo' sho' they knew they had to cause not one of them bitches could kick her ass one on one.

I loved living with all of my aunts, uncles and grandmother. I got my ass whipped a lot more, but I had everything I could ask for.

RIP Sabrina! Love, you cousin.

UNCLE TICK

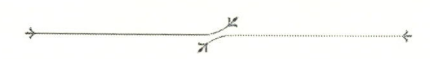

Uncle Tick is my mother's younger brother and I have always had a special type of uncle-nephew relationship with him. Auntie Dorothy was his wife. He had been an uncle and father to me. Unc sent for me to come and stay with them. Moms needed a helping hand. Auntie could use someone to help with the trash and go to the store. Unc also wanted me there to beat up them lil niggas that was constantly fucking with my cousins. I sho'nuff did beat all of them lil niggaz up that was ganging up on my cousins. After I kicked they ass Unc told'em every time yall fuck with someone in my family that's what's gon' happen. The parents came to him wanting to talk and he cursed all their asses out. He said, "when yo' son and 'nem was jumping on my nephews and 'nem' you didn't wanna talk, so why you wanna talk now?" He had me kickin' all of them lil niggaz ass that fucked with my family until them lil niggaz wanted to be they friends.

Uncle Tick and his wife Aunt Dorthy had three kids at the time: Dewone, Sharon, and lil Robert. While staying with them, I slept in the bed with Lil Robert. One night I peed in the bed and blamed it on Lil Robert. Sorry about that cuzo. I don't remember if yo' momma whooped yo' ass or not, but shit, I'm glad I had you to blame it on. You saved my ass.

During that time Auntie Lulu left with Cynthia and moved to California. She left her key to her project on South Eight with Uncle Tick. Man, that became the spot to bag up duffle bags of weed. I do mean duffle bags. I learned how to bag up pounds, half pounds, quarter pounds, ounces, half ounces, quarter ounces, dime bags, nickel bags, and roll joints. I stapled bags of weed until my fingers hurt. Real shit, I put in work for Unc. I was his runner. I dropped off pre-prepared brown paper sack to all his workers. I refuse to mention names. Yet, a lot of brothers that ended up being major, were put on in the game through Unc.

SOUTH EIGHTH

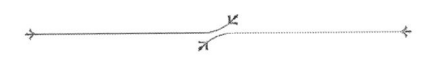

South Eighth was the #1 strip on that side of town back in those days. It was a lot of racist shit going on during those times too especially in East Nashville. Don't misunderstand me, racism was a bad, period! Just so happened, its head shined like the morning sun in East Nashville. The killing on South 5th in front of the workhouse going to J & J Liquor store started major shit. Whites were coming to South Eight to buy K-4's, get the pills, and just take off with the pills. So, the brothers with no pills started running off with the white boys' money. Some of the white boys came back and would just shoot whoever.

Pancake was killed in a mistaken identity situation. RIP Pancake. That shit hurt me badly. Pancake was a good dude. The killing of Pancake triggered a lot of shit. Everything changed on South Eighth after that. Shit just got crazy. So many whites were being shot and killed that cameras were placed on the light poles. South Eighth street was the first to have those cameras installed in Nashville. The police were stopping the whites on Shelby Street as soon as they turned on South Eighth, before they could come down the street. Turning them away, warning them of the dangers they faced coming over there to buy drugs. Times were booming on South Eighth, too. There were hangout spots all over: Dairy Dip, a new game room for the kids, and Disco Heaven, a night club, all opened. Money was flowing good. Niggas was getting new cars. The old heads were getting out of the way for the younger hustlers to take over. Shit was changing fast.

I had started getting real pussy by then. I was crazy about this girl named Janet. Man, she put that pussy on me one time and I couldn't handle it. She knew how to fuck already. She was my age but had been fucking grown men. The pussy was so wet, and the bitch was fucking me back so good, I came too fast. I never tried to fuck her again after that, but I never forgot how good that pussy was.

After her came Cathy. Cathy was sneaky. Sneaking and giving up the pussy while her mom was at work. We were doing it, but it wasn't like it was with Janet. Cathy wasn't really wet and easy to get in; and I didn't like it. I liked it the way Janet's pussy was. Little did I know,

Janet's pussy was open from doing a lot of fucking. She put that pussy on me back then, and I couldn't handle it.

Getting pussy too young always fuck up a young nigga. Once he starts fucking, can't nobody tell him shit. He gets to thinking with his dick, thinking he grown and shit. I really started fucking up. Skipping school, fighting teachers and shit. Uncle Tick had to send me back to mom's house because I got put out of school. I was glad to be back at mom's house because I could get away with' moe' shit. I hated them whippings that Uncle Tick and Auntie Dorthy had for a nigga; they were something serious. I did miss being with them afterwards because everything was better for me while living with them. But they were strict. They wanted to meet the girlfriend and their parent(s) type shit.

SPEAK TRUTH

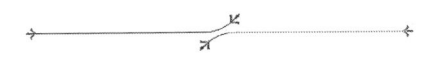

Feel me ya', I grew up in the hood, from a family of street hustlers yet, traditional as fuck. All my uncles married their high school sweethearts with marriages that lasted for 30 to 40 years. A few until death did them part! It is well known in our city streets that the men of our bloodline are providers. We take care of our shit! I am very proud to be a part of the Corley, Sawyers, Moody, Harris, Harrison, Jackson, French, Hawkins, Thompson, Carpenter and many more that are a part of the legacy of this family. I feel grateful to be a part of a bloodline of real men. Men who will correct yo' ass when you're wrong. Help you up, when you're down. Is on your team through whatever, as long as a nigga real. I am extremely proud of the boss nigga's that are my family. I was still in my teens when I was sentenced to life in prison. All my younger cousins were at least three years younger than me, specifically Lil T and Nate. However, by the time them nigga were sixteen; they became young millionaires, and they held me down. I mean, held me down for the 28 1/2 years I did straight. Shit don't get no realer!

Thank you, niggas
Yall my niggaz, nothing but love relatives!

MOMMY I'M BACK

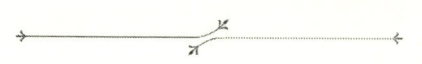

Going back to mom's meant east Nashville, Rock City, Panorama Apartments, a rat-infested apartment complex. When we first moved out there, in 1977, it wasn't that bad. It was fairly quiet, and an ok place. There was street, hood-thug, project raised niggaz that lived there, but everyone was low-key and not mixing. Our family changed the way things were over there and brought all the worst out with me being at the center of it all. We started having parties, gambling, and fighting. None of that was going on before we moved over there.

It took no time for almost everybody in the complex to know me, even the rental people. I stayed in some shit! At eleven years old, I was already a lil hit man for the family. I was about four feet eleven inches tall, about eighty-nine pounds with bricks in my pockets, and had to fight whoever about all my younger cousins. Man, I was serious, serious, serious about fuckin' a nigga up for fuckin' with my family. I 'clare fo' cheese an crackers I was not trying to be tough, or trying to go for bad, but I kicked ass coming up. I was a fighting lil muthafucka, I knew how to fight; sprang first and didn't stop. Just beat a nigga down for real. If the beat down doesn't do, stab'em or hit'em in the head with a bat or something. Ya' I was fucked up like that in the head. Hurt people, hurt people. I was still hurting badly over the lack of love and attention that I wasn't getting from my dad. I didn't know it then, but that was the cause of a lot of the shit I was going through, lashing out.

I first got put out of school in the fifth grade for constantly fighting. My mother had to take me before the Tennessee Board of Education to be informed that I couldn't go to any other Metropolitan School. I was sent to an alternative school for "bad ass kids." It was called The Meharry Achievement Center, located at the Meharry Hospital complex. They went to school all year round. I didn't like it that much. But that got - damn short - bus that I had to ride to school did it for me. It was summertime and all the kids in the complex were out when the short bus pulled up to let me out. Man, they pointed fingers at me and laughed at me hard as hell. I ran straight in the house and didn't come back out that day. That was the last day I rode the "short bus." "Fuck that bus and fuck that school. I ain't going back no moe", I said. My momma said, "what you just say?" I repeated myself loud and clear, I said, "I ain't going back to that school no moe. Fuck that school and fuck that bus. I ain't riding that bus no moe.

At that point moms was tired. I had already lived with uncles, aunts, and gran- mommy. They didn't know what to do with me. I was given tutoring. I passed through a tutor and was placed in Litton Jr. High. I was in school for maybe a month and got put out for smacking a teacher. Momma told me again, "You lucky they didn't kill you for hitting that white woman." Man, I didn't know! She talked that shit, and I smacked that bitch. That was the end of school for me.

During that time, I was selling and smoking weed, drinking, driving, getting pussy, and always fighting. My cousins, T and Nate, were my closest cousins, because they were only three years younger than me. They used to love being around me and hanging out with me, but Uncle Bally wasn't having much of that. Unc knew I was into too much shit. I was his runner at the time and although it was cool for me, that shit wasn't cool for them. Them niggaz was being raised to be a lot more respectful and I was calling niggaz mommas a bitch and then beat the son up for trying to defend his momma. Yeah, I was fucked up.

Nothing else was said about me going to school. I never attended the 8th grade, and nobody cared. I was glad. Fuck school! I lost interest when that white teacher tried to convince me that all black people had ever been, were slaves. I wasn't educated, but I did have a living spirit in my heart that rejected that bullshit. I was excited about not going to school. I would sleep most of the day and be up all night, in the "Ramaz " drinking, smoking and shooting dice. The police were constantly breaking up the dice game. So, I convinced my Auntie, May'ran, to let us start shooting dice in the house. I was running the game, but she was the House Lady collecting the craps. That became a part of our hustle. I was already her runner. Picking up her weed from Uncle Bally and selling it for her too. We were partners in the hustle, together, and we were coming up. Doing really good. All the niggaz that shot dice started coming to gamble. Shit was going good with the dice game until this nigga name Lester decided to start some shit. He was high on them T's and Blues and was strapped. He fucked up and chose the wrong nigga to start shit with. He pulled the gun up, but Yancy was on his ass. One shot was fired in the ceiling because Yancy was on his ass so fast. We had two refrigerators in the kitchen at the time so, we pushed both refrigerators over on top of them. Then, Yancy yelled, "I got him, I got him!" We pulled the refrigerators up and Yancy dragged the nigga Lester outside to the high porch. They both had their hands on the gun. Yancy had locked his finger over top of Lester's finger. Both of their fingers were on the trigger. Once outside on the porch, Yancy started beating Lester's ass badly. He beat Lester until Lester let go of the gun and guess who grabbed it? You guessed it right, it was me. That's how I came to be in possession of my first 38. It was 1979, and I was 13 years old.

The next day I was approached by Lester about giving him his gun back. First, I denied having the gun. He refused to accept me saying I didn't have the gun because he saw me when I grabbed it. So, the nigga started talking shit about beating my ass and shit. I ended up having to pull the gun out on the nigga and let him know that all he was gon' get was the bullets up out that muthafucka. I went into the house and told Auntie May'ran what happened. Auntie told me, "Be careful and watch myself when you are outside. Make sure you keep it on you and if that nigga even acts like he gon' try something, you better shoot that muthafucka." I said, "Yes, ma'am!" Trust me, that nigga was gon' get every bullet in that muthafucka fuckin' with me. I was in love with that muthafucka before I even shot anybody. I knew then that my fighting days were over. I couldn't wait to pop me a nigga. Just give me a reason nigga! Just give me a reason!!!

CROSSROADS

The very first day that we moved to Panorama tha "Ramaz" was the day that my life started to change for the worse. I started smoking weed, cigarettes, drinking liquor and beer.

WELCOME HOME GRAN-DADDY

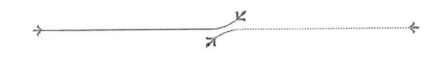

My Grand-daddy is my Great-granddaddy to me, my mother's Grand-daddy, my grandmother's father Ovrey Corley. I remember Gran-daddy, as everybody called him, from back around 1971 or 1972. I was five or six years old at the time and I remember him coming around for a few days or so and disappear. We were in University Court at the time and when he would show up, he would always have them orange slices candy. He would always give me some plus some change out of his lil pouch, the change pouch you had to squeeze together to open. He also always had bread and applesauce.

Gran-daddy was a kind-hearted man. I say that because he always offered everyone some of whatever he had. He always had a jug of that nasty ass sulfur water. Man, he gave me a drink of that shit one time, at six years old, it had me spitting and shit. His ass was pointing his finger and laughing at me. It was all my fault because I begged him for a drink. He told me it wasn't regular water, still I begged. Finally, he said, "Ok, now I told ya" and gave me a drink. Man damn, I spit and spit and spit. He was just pointing his finger at me and laughing. I still remember that smile of his as he laughed.

Gran-daddy was a very handsome man. He was mixed with part Indian, and you could see it in him clearly. With his golden-brown skin, high cheekbones and always clean shaven. Gran-daddy always wore suits. That was the Negro side of him. He was a drifter, a serious walker. He traveled on foot all over Nashville. My brother's and I are the same way. One day Gran-daddy was crossing the street on Nolensville Road and was hit by a car. Gran-daddy was 75 or a little older at the time of the accident. It broke both of his legs, one of his arms, and two of his ribs. The doctors said, "he would never walk again." They didn't know who Ovrey Corley was. Gran-daddy called my mother; my mother had a close relationship with her Gran-daddy. She went and got him and brought him home to take care of him.

Keep in mind, at the time we were living in the "Ramaz" with four little bedrooms. My moms and Auntie May'ran had their room, but he had a hospital bed, so he had to have his own room. That left one room for five boys. Picture that shit! Man, lookin' back on that makes me understand how a nigga was so fucked up mentally. One bathroom in a house of ten people. Everybody in the house had a reason to have an attitude every day. Now I understand better why there was so much built-up anger and hostility in everyone. Our living conditions created that shit.

Anyway, my mother took on a major responsibility with Gran-daddy. She had to do it all. He couldn't do anything for himself. He would shit and piss on himself daily, and he hated having to depend on my mother so much. I used to spend time with him every day. He got used to me coming to his room; he would be waiting on me, would light up with a big smile as soon as I entered the room. My mother would be in the room sometimes and soon as she saw me, I heard her say, "here he go now." Letting me know he was asking about me. He shared his innermost deepest thoughts, feelings and memories from his past with me. He always cried when he spoke of his mother, brothers, and sisters. He never mentioned his father. The story he constantly repeated was "them white muthafuckin' son-of-a-bitches killed'em all. He poisoned 'em all' an put the poison in the milk. I told'em not to drink that milk,' I told'em." He would cry every time he told me that story. I told my mother the things he was telling me. My mother told me "don't listen to him, he just talking jibber-jabber. He is old." I told my mother "no he's not talking jibber-jabber, he knows what he's talking about, and you need to listen to him mommy." I could hear the truth in his words. It all made sense to me. It explained why no one in the family knew anything about his mother, father, brothers or sisters.

He recuperated from his injuries and got strong. Never walk again that doctor said, he was wrong. Gran-daddy started walking after about a year and a half. Once he was able to walk again Aunt Hazel, his daughter, came and got him and took him to Ohio. About a year later he died.

RIP Grandaddy

PATRICK GREER AKA PAT

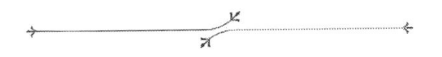

I had come to know Patrick Greer at around 10 years old, when I was staying with my grandmother at 853 South Eight Street. His big brother, Vincent Greer, was my Uncle Jimmy aka W.C., pronounced double C, partner. Pat and I ended up getting cool during that time around late 75 early 76. One day coming home from school, Pat and I stopped by his house and found his mother dead in the tub. Supposedly, "she had drowned." A few weeks later Pat and his brothers moved. His big brother Vincent was still hanging out with WC and coming to my grandmother's house. Him and Aunt Jackie have kids together. Vincent, would have Pat with him from time to time so he and I would hang out.

In 1977, we moved to the "Ramaz" and Pat, came to our building, building G, to help us move in. He lived in building A. Once we finished moms told us to go outside and let her get her house in order. So, we went to Pat's house in building A. Man, that nigga had Jack Daniel's, Bull beer, cigarettes and weed. I had never touched cigarettes or weed before then. I had tasted some liquor but had never really drunk any. I ended up getting fucked up, bad, and went home fucked up. Lucky for me everybody was tired from all the moving. Moms had bought Kentucky fried chicken, so I ate it and went to bed. My drug and alcohol use started on that day. I can honestly say that it changed my whole life. From that day forward even up until this very day, March 15, 2022, drugs and alcohol remains a part of my life.

It was summertime when we moved in, so Pat and I hung out every day. He didn't always have food in the house, but he always had weed, beer, liquor, and cigarettes. I would get food out of my house for Pat. My mother saw me get food one time and called us both into the house. She asked me, "why you giving him our food?" I said, "because he hungry momma, and he haven't had nothing to eat." My mother started asking questions about his mother and stuff. He told my mother everything. From then on, he was welcome to eat in our house.

We were still hanging out at his house every day until one day he told me to wait on the high porch. He went inside and when he came back to the door, he told me to be quiet as we snuck to his room.

Once in his room he said his daddy was home and he was in the room asleep. Everything in the house started to change once his daddy came home. The oldest brother was Rudy. He moved out first. Then Randy moved out. Eventually, Vincent and Rudolph slowly stopped coming home. None of them cared much for their daddy. I was hearing the arguments and shit, but I wasn't putting it all together at the time. One day after school, Pat told me to walk down to his house with him first. So, we passed by my house and walked down to his house. We got to his house and found the front door cracked open. We stepped inside and there was water all over the floor, the same as it was at his mother's house that day. We went to the kitchen, then the bathroom. We found his daddy dead in the tub with the water still running. Pat was placed in a group home, and I stayed in contact with him. After a few years he started getting passes to come home for 8 hours on the weekends. I would pick him up and take him back. He was at this place called the Cumberland House located on 12th Ave and Wedgewood, on the Southside of Nashville, Tennessee. Going to visit him is how I met Candy. During that time, I was half ass grown. My new partner was Alfonzo Burns, RIP. I was also hanging out with my big brother Fudd, Uncle WC, Dee Dee, Tony Smith aka Pretty Tony, RIP, Pasha, and Ronald Newsome. I was running weed for my Uncle Bally Jones and Uncle Tick, as well as selling weed for my auntie May'ran. I had a car that Dee Dee had given to me that I was hiding from my mother, but she knew I had it.

My big brother, Edmund Deon Corley, aka Fudd, and my Uncle Jimmy Glenn Sawyers were the same age. From what legend says, my mother and grandmother were in the hospital at the same time at some point. Anyway, at a young age I had the blessing of being able to roll with my big brother and Uncle WC. RIP to both of y'all. Dam my niggas really gone. My big brother Fudd was a "Pretty Boy-Lover Boy" as a lot of females would say. At 16, he had 2 cars, 5 girlfriends, and 3 baby mommas who had their child by him around about the same time. He was also the apple of my momma's eye. My mother had him around 14 or 15 years old. So, she really spoiled him. He was my favorite brother. He was very protective of me and I of him. I looked up to my big brother because he was a real big brother to me. He always showed me so much love. He took me with him all the time. He bought me clothes, let me drive his cars, and mess with the girls he messed with younger sisters. We double dated. He took me out to eat and to the drive-in movies with him, his girlfriend, and the lil sister. I even went to the Era, with him, WC, Vincent, and Eric House. Even then WC always gave me the gun. Somehow, I always ended up with the gun.

South Eight was the track at that time. Plenty niggas on South Eight was getting they shit through my Uncle Bally aka Bally Jones and Uncle Tick. I was in the center of it all. I loved being with my big brother Fudd! He wouldn't let me sale weed on the street. But he said nothing about me having the gun. I would watch all their backs as WC, Fudd, and the crew sold they weed.

Remember, my nigga WC was my uncle, and my partner. We were close as hell. He was the youngest and wildest of his brothers. The same as I was, the youngest and wildest out of my brothers too. Unc was a gangsta and at a young age I had to put in work with Unc. Unc stayed in some shit! He was quick to pop off and pop a nigga ass. However, the niggas on South Eight respected and had love for the family. Therefore, we didn't have a lot of problems. I used to roll with Unc, late night. He had a gold and brown 1978 Monte Carlo SS. He stayed strapped, on that gin, and ready for whatever. He would disrespect a muthafucka' fa' no reason whatsoever. He was with tha' shit. One time this nigga name Darrly C pushed my brother Jr. through the Pantry Store window, the store located behind the "Ramaz." Unc came through and pistol whipped tha' nigga. This woman who family wanted to go for being bad, had nothing to do with the shit, decides to aim a shotgun toward me and Unc. He opened fire on tha' bitch. All you could hear was screams and muthafuckas' yelling, "call tha' police." Unc took off up Cahal Street and I was right behind him, but he had about a half of a block on me. We both saw the police pull into the "Ramaz" and muthafuckas' were pointing in our direction as we were running up Cahal Street. I saw Unc throw the gun. I ran straight to the landing spot of the gun and in one smooth motion I picked up the gun, ran across the street, laid in the grass for a few minutes, and watched the police search for the gun. I got up and ran to Uncle Bally's house. I saved Unc's ass. That wouldn't be the last time.

About six months later it was Unc's Blood Day, as he would call it if he was still here. He decided to have a B-Day party at our house, in the "Ramaz". Shit was going good. The party was jumping. Everybody was enjoying the moment. All of a sudden, this nigga name Rick grabbed Uncs' wife Rena, by the arm. The nigga wanted to dance with Rena. She had already turned the nigga down, and tried to walk away from him. Unc and I both seen what was going on and approached Rick, to make him let Rena arm go. The nigga got aggressive, so we got aggressive and forced the nigga up out of the house. We went back to enjoying the party. A spirit caught my attention to the front door. No soon as I got to the door, I saw Rick with a shot gun in hand coming up the steps. I screamed, "He got a gun" as I try to move people out of the way so that I could close the front door. But he was able to stop the door from closing with the barrel of the shotgun. He pulled the trigger hitting 3 people or more with buckshot's. Unc, Fudd, and Kenny Wayne all grabbed guns and tried to catch the nigga. He ran into an apartment in the next building. They shot the apartment up hoping to hit the nigga. We came out the next day to find the apartment empty. They had moved out in the middle of the night.

CANDY GIRL

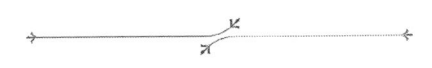

New Edition had just dropped their song Candy Girl and I had just met Candy. Candy stole my heart. It was that love at first sight type of shit. I don't know how but instantly upon laying eyes on her my muthafuckin heart just melted for her ass. Lol!

I went to pick up Pat, something I had done several times on Saturday around 12 noon. I was heading inside the building to sign Pat, out when I noticed her. I just looked at her, like DAMN! Pat, said "what's wrong with you?" I asked, "who is that?" He said, "that's Candy." I asked him, "can I talk to her." He said, " ya" and called her over. I started talking to her and told her I wanted her to be my girlfriend. She said, "ok." As we were talking Pat came out of the building ready to go. He said, "come on man I'm ready to go." Then he said, "you can sign her out too. She got a pass, she just ain't got nobody to sign her out." So, I signed her out. We went straight to mom's house. As soon as mom saw Candy, she started asking questions. Pat and I left Candy in the living room being interrogated by moms. When we came back about an hour later, moms had Candy helping her in the kitchen. They were laughing and shit, the energy between them was good. I walked into the kitchen and just stood there. Moms looked at me and said, "we will be done in a minute." I must have been looking anxious. I said nothing and went to my room. About 10 minutes later Candy came to my room. And I was on her ass. I was straight thinking with my dick. I closed the door and as soon as I did; moms come knockin on tha' door, talkin bout "open up this doe', what 'cha call yourself doing?" Man, I was mad as a muthafucka'. I was cursing mom's out, under my breath; as I grabbed Candy, by the hand and headed for the door.

We went and just sat in the car. I wasn't saying nothing, just sitting there mad as hell. Then Candy said, "you look good even when you're mad. But you look better when you're smiling. You're going to get all the pussy you want from me, just be cool." She kissed me on the lips. We talked in the car for a while. She told me all about how she was molested by her stepdad. That's how she ended up in the group home. Her mother was black, and her daddy was white. I met her real daddy years later at the Tennessee State Penitentiary aka tha' Walls in 1989.

She told me her mother had given her away as a baby. She kept running away because she was being molested by the man who wife had adopted her and about all the white men who paid her for sex. After we talked, I no longer wanted to just have sex with Candy. I wanted to protect her, love her, and take Care of her. I remember how it felt as we held hands and she leaned her head on the headrest and looked at me and ask me, "is all you want is some pussy or do you want me? I responded, "I want you." She said, "do you promise to always love me no matter what and never leave me? My dumb ass said, "I promise to always love you and to never leave you. We hugged each other and held each other. I heard a whimper from her, and I leaned back to look at her face. I saw the tears in her eyes, and it brought tears to mine. We just held each other and cried together. We made a bond that day. And I was committed to the promises I made her.

    I was able to see Candy on Tuesday's, Thursday's, and she had her 8 hours passes on Saturday's. We talked on the phone a lot. Candy was planning to run away from the group home. I tried to talk her out of it, but her mind was already made up. I didn't hear from Candy for about 4 days. One day Pat called and left a message for me to pick him and Candy up on South Eight. I picked'em up and took'em to mom's house. Off the top, soon as we walked through the door moms let it be known that Candy couldn't stay there. Moms explained about her age and that she could go to jail for having her because she was a runaway. Pat was able to stay because moms had signed temporary custody of him until his 18th birthday. So, I left the house with Candy thinking of where we could go. We were sitting in the car when Ms. Dorthy, Alfonzo's, mother walked up and asked me to take her to the store. I pulled up at H.G. Hill and Ms. Dorthy asked Candy to go in the store with her to help her out. When they came back to the car Candy got in the back seat. She was smiling hard as hell. A real happy smile! She said, "we stayin' at Ms. Dorthy's tonight." Fonzo was in Spencer Youth Center for some dumb shit that we had got caught doin' together, but my criminal record wasn't fuck up like his at the time so I went home. He was sent up the river! So, Ms Dorthy said we could sleep in Fonzo room. We stopped at the Pantry Store and got me some beer and cigarettes. Then we went to Ms. Dorthy's. That night was the very first night that I had had sex with Candy.

    The next morning, we woke up to the police beating on the door. They were looking for Candy and wanted to search for her. Ms.

Dorthy refused to let them search her house. Once they left, she let us know that Candy had to go. So, we left. I was trying to figure out where the fuck were we going to go. I couldn't just leave Candy in the streets by herself. We left. I stopped at the store and this white dude named Fat Tim pulled up. Fat Tim was a white dude who had the privilege of growing up around us in tha' "Ramaz"; who also used to buy weed from me. He immediately noticed Candy, and asked, "who is that?"

"That's Candy," I said.

"Do you think she will give me some if I pay'ha?"

I said, "man that's my girl."

He laughed and said, "damn man I'm'a pay'ha!"

I told Candy what he said. She looked at me and said, "I'll do it if you want me to!" Naw bitch, I don't want you too. But shit I knew that sometimes you gotta do what 'cha gotta do. So, I told Fat Tim, she's willing to do it if we can stay with him for a few days. He agreed so I followed Fat Tim to where he lived.

He lived on Fatherland Street, and it was one big building with a lot of little apartments inside. The apartment was so small that the kitchen table was a square piece of wood that you pulled down from the wall. Tim and I sat and talked while Candy went to shower. When Candy came out of the bathroom, I felt a little fucked up about knowing that Fat Tim was about to fuck her. Fat Tim was in a hurry. So much so that he rushed her to go into his room and shit. I grabbed my beer and headed for the door.

"Where you going? You're not leaving me here with him, are you? If you're not staying, I'm not staying. I'm leaving with chu,' "I'm not leaving, I'm just going to set in the car for a minute.

"Are you sure you're alright with me doing it? Because if you're not I won't do it!"

I said, "naw I'm cool with it. I'm just going to the car for a minute."

Really, I was fucked up about the shit. My heart hurt a little bit about the situation. But, Candy had to have a place to stay. I knew all about hoes. My auntie Pam was a Madame. I had lived with her and a house full of hoes. My auntie used to make all of them hoes give me money. She told me to say, "pay a pimp" as I go from hoe-to-hoe with my hands out. But I had feeling for Candy. My feelings were caught up in tha' mix, muthafuckin' feelings was hurt badly! I loved Candy! And it was more than just being in love with her.

My heart hurt for her.

Over her.

Because of her.

Yet and still, I was committed to always being there for her no matter what. As I had promised. Candy, knew that!

Every day I would walk over to South Eight, to hang with my Uncle Tick to see what I could do to make a few dollars. Auntie Dorthy would almost always send me to the store and pay me a few dollars for going. Uncle Tick would let me sale a few bags to get a few dollars. During that time my nigga WC was in the workhouse. Once Jimmy wasn't around, my big brother Fudd and Vincent didn't hang on South Eight anymore. Lonnie Greenlee use to be on my ass about being on the street like I was. Rick Tick, Shoney, Victor P., Silver, Lil Enod, and Poochie Pointer, RIP, was a couple years older than me. They stayed on my ass about me running to cars because of how white boys had started shooting niggaz that ran to the cars.

South Eight got so bad, the police jumped out of ambulance, fire trucks, school buses, or whatever. So, we all started hanging in the bridge ways, and made the white boys come to the bridge ways. We were able to get away from the police because we would hit the bridge ways on they ass. So, the chief of police had the mayor authorize the Metropolitan Housing Authority to put bars up in the middle of the bridge ways. South Eight was the hottest projects in Nashville, at the time, because of all the white boys being killed. That's why Unc, didn't want me on the street.

You Gotta Let a Hoe Be a Hoe

Candy and I had literally moved in with Fat Tim. I would go over to South Eighth to make $20 or $30 dollars a day for food and shit. Candy was supposed to stay in the house, but Candy was a hoe. She was a hoe to her heart! I get to the house one day, and Candy is gone. I was pacing the floor when I just happened to walk by the window and noticed a car had stopped in front of the building. The passenger side door opens and it's Candy getting out of the car. As soon as I saw it was Candy, I ran out of the apartment, going down the steps as fast as

I could. I get to the street just in time enough to see that it was an older white man dropping her off. I smacked the shit out of her.

"Bitch you wanna be a hoe and fuck around on me."

I grabbed the bitch by the hair and drug her ass up the steps. I got her ass in tha' house and beat her ass. My heart changed toward Candy that day. She was no longer the Candy that I loved and wanted all to myself. She became the Candy that I loved and hated because I knew that I would never have her all to myself. I told Candy that day that since you wanna be a hoe, you gon' be a real hoe! So, I went and hollered at my nigga Dee Dee.

Dee Dee was a rider, my nigga, he got me my first car. I looked up to Dee Dee. Our partnership started the day that his black ass was in handcuffs in the backseat of a police car in tha' "Ramaz." Everybody was just standing around looking at his ass. He and I made eye to eye contact, and he said with his lips to open tha' door and let him out. The officer was nearby but wasn't paying attention. So, I opened tha' door and let him out. We both took off running. He had me chop the cuffs in half with an axe. I was scared I was gon' hit his ass. That nigga said, "man just do it." I did. From that day forward, he would pick me up to ride with him. He is the one that really taught me how to drive. Dee Dee is the one that gave me my first car. He is the one that Pasha, a big brother from another mother, was try'na keep me away from. He knew Dee Dee was a real hot boy. He knew that he stayed in some crazy shit, like shootouts and shit. He knew the police were always looking for Dee Dee for something, and he was trying to keep me away from that shit. After I cut the cuffs in half. He went into the house. When he came back out, the cuffs were off. We got in one of his other cars and went to Krystals. We ate and then went to the "Ramaz" to get his other car that he had to run off and left. He pulled up in front of the car, gave me the keys, and told me to follow him. I had driven before, but not by myself. I drove the car to his house, parked it, and got in the car with him. He gave me $20, bought me a beer, a pack of cigarettes, and dropped me off at the Pantry Store behind the "Ramaz".

From that day forward that nigga had me in all -kinds-of-shit. I was the driver. But many times, I had to shoot to save his ass. 2 or 3 times I damn near got killed fuckin' with him. That nigga had me doing drive and pop-ups. I would drive up and he would pop up from the back seat and shoot tha' nigga. He would do some shit in one of his cars and weeks later I would be driving tha' car and niggas would shoot the car up, thinking it was him. Although he would tell me not to go in certain areas, I was excited to be driving. I was everywhere in his cars.

I pulled up at Dee Dee house but didn't recognize his car. He was in a different car. He came outside and told me where to park. Him, Candy, and I went in his house. I told him the business, and he told me about the truck stop. That night we went to the truck stop. Them white men went crazy for Candy. On the real for real though, Candy was bad. High yellow. Full lips. Breast. Hips and Azz. She was about five feet five and about 148 pounds. Young, ripe, and slightly bow-legged. She had that real snapper. That bitch pussy snapped back like she had never been fucked before. I didn't fuck Candy often because I despised her for selling my pussy. But the few times that I did, her pussy would pop like she was being busted out for the first time. I hated that Candy was selling my pussy. I never wanted her to be doing that, but she had learned that lifestyle way before me!

Damn, Damn, Damn

Candy ended up being taken into custody at the truck stop. She was sent back to juvey. I was back at Fat Tim's apartment. We both were sad as hell. About a week or so later, I went back to the "Ramaz", just to find out that we had been put out because of that shooting. Moms had found a house out south on Wharf Ave. I hated University Court. I had grown up in those projects and I seriously hated that shit. But, after a week or so of Fat Tim and I both being all sad and shit, I had to go. I hated that I was leaving. But I had to go.

Bad Decision

That was the worst decision ever. I hated them projects. All the killings and shit I seen coming up in University Court fucked me up. I went back out south straight on some I'm gonna kill as many of these niggas as I could kill, type shit. My mental state was internally scarred from my days of growing up in that shit. To me University Court was a killing field. And I was ready to kill as many as I could kill, before one of them killed me.

I became trigger happy as soon as I came back to University Court. We lived at 109 Wharf Ave, right across the street from UC. I wouldn't even go in the projects at first. Until one day my mother wanted me to walk her up to my grandmothers in the U of UC. As we were walking, I saw a few girls that I liked coming up. A lot of people were happy to see me. Still, I was missing my niggas from the "Ramaz" and they were missing me too. They all started coming out South. Pasha, Ronald Newsome, and Dee Dee. WC had got out of the work house and was coming out south to see his mommy, my grandmother. Terry, Jimmy and I started running together.

My Nigga Terry
RIP Bruh

I met Terry during the days I was in tha' "Ramaz." He and I didn't really fuck with each other, as far as hangin' together was concerned. But we recognized each other and were on cool terms. Terry had his crew of cool ass niggas. They all were dancers and shit. I mean they were serious dancers. Terry and his crew was on a professional level with the dancing shit because they were on cable tv poppin and breakin! He danced with the Pop-Alone-Kid. That nigga had the style, the look, and his ass had the moves. The nigga was good.

Terry's lil brother, Reggie aka Goo Goo, was a part of the lil crew of shoplifters that I was hung out with sometimes as a side hustle. I couldn't steal for shit. I just didn't have it in me. But them other young niggaz was good at it. I was good at selling stolen merchandise. I would always make sure I had at least enough money to give everybody $5 for bus fare and something to eat. We would walk to Gallatin Road, from the "Ramaz," and catch the bus all the way to Rivergate Mall. We would walk back, hitting every store on the way back, stealing everything we could. I say we because I was with them, but I wasn't stealing shit. It just wasn't in me. One time we went into a store and soon as we got into the store, they started following us. I walked back to the front of the store, to separate myself from them niggas. I was at the counter by myself. I looked behind the counter and saw one of them green money bags. I grabbed the bag and eased on out the door. I got down the street, went into the alley and opened it, and saw the money. I just stuffed it in my pocket and jumped on the next bus going home. I didn't say nothing to not one of them niggaz. I just got on down. When they made it home, they were saying that they thought I had got caught. They said they were looking for me, waiting on me, and when I didn't show up, they got on the next bus and came home. They were excited to see me, especially that nigga Wayne Gross. My nigga still til this very day, noticed me first.

I was the one that sold everybody's shit. Them niggaz always had a lot of shit. I would take all the shit to my Uncle Bally. It would be 6 or 7 hundred dollar's worth of shit. I would sale it all to Unc. For 2 hundred and an ounce of weed. I gave them niggaz 25 dollars each and a lil weed. I kept 100 and almost a half-ounce of weed. I would get Newsome to get us two quarts of beer and we would get high. And then I would start a dice game and win almost all of the money. That shit happened all during the summer.

It was during that time, prior to Candy coming into my life, that I was sent to Spencer Youth Center. Spencer was a detention center for delinquent kids who weren't goin' to school. Man, I stayed fighting in that muthafucka'. I could have only done 3 months, but I ended up doing 6 months around late 81 or early 82.

Big Fonzo

Alfonzo Burns RIP

First, Fonzo went to Spencer and he stayed for about 4 months. At that time my cousin Sabrina Corley was staying with us in the "Ramaz". Fonzo and I were partners. I was sneaking Fonzo into the crib, he and Sabrina were sexing. That's how she got pregnant with lil Fonzo, Alfonzo Corley. RIP, luv Relative. Sabrina and I were always close. We were only a year or so apart, and we lived in different houses at different times together. Soon as Sabrina got pregnant, Fonzo ended up going to Taft Youth Center. It was during that time that I met Candy. Remember, Ms. Dorthy, RIP, Alfonzo's mother let me and Candy stay for that one night. Candy, got caught up at the truck stop a few days later.

I Had To Go And See About Candy

Candy already knew mom's address and phone number out south. Her case worker made contact with my mother, in search of me. It was a week or so after Candy had got caught that I moved to moms at 109 Wharf Ave. Moms gave me the man's name and number. I called him. He was seriously happy to hear from me. He explained to me Candy's circumstances. He pleaded with me to please meet with him at the juvey detention center. He already had it approved for me to visit with Candy. I was refusing to go. Thinking it was a trick. He literally begged me.

He said, "please, come and see about Sandy," Candy's real name. "She doesn't have anyone else. She has been through so much, and you are her only hope. All she is doing is screaming and hollering and crying for you. I don't know why, but that girl loves you. If you care about her, as she believes you do, you will come and see her. I don't think she has ever needed anyone in her life, as much as she needs you right now."

I still believed the folks were trying to trick me. Yet, my heart made me go see about Candy. They locked us in a room together, and I stayed in that room with Candy until she fell asleep in my arms. We cried together for what seemed like hours. We laughed a little. But, really inside we both were sad as hell. Candy made me promise that I would wait for her. And I made her that promise. Candy had my heart, and nothing could stop my love for her.

She was gone for about a month. Fat Tim came out south one day looking for me to hang out with. We kicked it for a while and then he convinced me to ride back out east with him with the promise of dropping me back off out south whenever I wanted him too. It was around 7 o'clock on a Friday night, and I was ready to be around people. Fat Tim was tired of being in that apartment by himself. I was telling him to drop me back off. He kept saying, "man you gotta stay here tonight." He was laughing, but I was serious. I was ready to go right muthafuckin' then.

I told Tim, "Man look, I'm serious. I'm ready to go right now." "I'm serious too. I ain't taking you back out there!" He said.

I snapped up with tha' pistol I had and upside his head I went. It fucked him up when I hit him the first time. He was saying something when I hit his ass again. He fell to the floor and balled up, covering his head with his arms folded up over his head. He was crying and shit. I had clocked out. I made him get his ass up. I took his car keys. Made his ass walk to the car and put his ass in the trunk. I drove out south with him in the trunk.

I was getting off the interstate on Second Ave, going straight across when the trunk came up. I pulled over as Fat Tim came up out of the trunk. I shot the gun in the ground toward his feet, and he stopped. Cars was coming and people was looking as I made his ass get back in the trunk. I made it to moms house and saw my brother James, aka Heart attack. Him and Fat Tim were cool too. Remember, Fat Tim came up in the "Ramaz" with us. The only white boy. We all fucked with Fat Tim, he just fucked up by playing with me.

I gave my brother James the keys and told him to let Fat Tim out of the trunk.

He said, "let who of the trunk?"

"Fat Tim."

"Fat Tim? What Fat Tim doing in the trunk?"

"I made him get in the trunk."

"Man, I KNOW you ain't got no Fat Tim in no trunk!"

"Open the got damn trunk and let tha' man out tha' trunk, nigga, damn!"

He opened the trunk and when he saw Fat Tim he shook his head, looked at me and said, "you know I'ma tell momma on you." I told him, "I don't give a damn and went to the projects to hang out. I didn't know Fat Tim went and took a warrant out on me for auto theft, robbery, assault with a deadly weapon, and kidnapping.

I'm coming Candy, I'm coming!

About a week later, I was at the house when the phone rang. It was Candy telling me to come and get her. She was on south eight again. I was broke as hell. I went to my aunt Jackie for some money. She only had food stamps and gave me a 5-dollar food stamp. I had my lil brother Paul Ray, my mother adopted Paul Ray around 1975 when he was six months old, and his lil friends to cash in the food stamps for me. I went up in the U and started a dice game. In 20 minutes, I hit for $118. I called a cab and went to go get Candy. She lit up when I called her name from that cab. Niggaz on south eight that knew me was like, "dam nigga you came in a cab." They said, "she been bragging about you coming." She was smiling and talking shit. She said, "I told y'all my baby was coming to get me."

Candy wasted no time getting back to doing what she liked, selling pussy. She would pop up with guns, rings, and plenty of money for me. It was hoes on the strip telling me that I had a gold mine in Candy. If I would make her stop "flat backing" and letting niggaz just freak her and shit. I had a real pimp that tried to get me to sale Candy to him. I didn't understand that shit. But it was good for him that he knew I was regarded with that pistol because I would have gunned his ass down about Candy. I loved Candy, unconditionally. She was my Candy no matter how many niggaz she fucked or how many dicks she sucked or whatever. I was never her pimp. I was someone who she loved wholeheartedly, as wholeheartedly as her heart would allow. She knew I loved her the same way. I accepted Candy, for all of who she was. I accepted her as a hoe. And expected her to be a hoe.

One day my big brother Fudd came to me and said, "Lil Bruh don't be mad at me, but I wanna fuck Candy. Bad!" He said, "I been tryna pay her, but she said she can't do it unless you say it's alright." I told Candy, it was cool. He paid her. She gave the money to me. I gave it back to him.

Bad decisions always cost a nigga

I fucked up when I did that shit to Fat Tim. That was just straight muthafuckin' crazy on my part. I was driving a 1982 Bonneville and I didn't know the car had been stolen. I was stopped by the police and was taken to juvey. I was still released but was informed that I had an up-and-coming court date for the charges I had mentioned earlier. My lawyer did all he could to stop those other cases from being handed over to the grand jury. The deal was for me to turn myself in on October 2nd, 1983, and be released after my 18th birthday.

I turned myself in according to the date agreed upon. I was sent to Spencer Youth Center again. All the CO's there remembered me from the first time I was there. I was doing good, at first. Dee Dee, Candy, Fudd, and moms came to visit. One day I looked up and saw my big brother James coming through the door. That shit hurt me bad. Although James is my big brother and way bigger than me, I ended up kicking this niggas ass named King about fuckin' with him. It would take my big brother to tell you how that shit really went down. In the end, I was sent to Taft Youth Center, the penitentiary for teenagers

Taft was nothing like Spencer Youth Center. It was a pre-prison ride. Taft got yo' ass ready for the penitentiary. You had cigarettes. Weed. Free world clothes. Cash money. Your own tv, the same as it was in prison. You had to work. Your family could send you packages. Fights happened daily, especially with them Memphis niggas. I ended up hitting a nigga in the head with the milk ball, that round ball like handle on the milk box like what we had in school. I busted that nigga head real good. Put a dent in that muthafucka'. Dee Dee and Candy came to see me even at Taft. Taft was located deep in the back woods of East Tennessee. Candy and I fucked and everything. I could tell that Dee Dee had already fucked Candy, but I didn't give a fuck. Dee Dee, was my nigga for real. That time went fast. And in no time I was heading home.

I'm Free

I had to catch the greyhound to get home. I was coming through University Court from the top end when I happened to stop this girl to ask if she knew my Auntie Jackie. The girl turned out to be Tina. She showed me where my auntie Jackie stayed. I told Tina to wait on me for a minute while I went in my auntie's house. Auntie Jackie had the keys to moms' house and $50 for me. I left my suitcase at my auntie's house and went with Tina. I was on Tina's ass. I had her blushing and shit, and 15 or 20 minutes later I was all up in her pussy.

Tina was crazy about me too. She wanted to have my baby. I had put the dick on her without me even realizing it. She remembered me from being out there before I went to Pikeville. Her brother's, Bar and Dirk, use to hang with my brother Fudd and 'nem. I hung out with Tina, for a good while. Tina and I were walking through the projects heading to moms on Wharf Ave when Candy saw me. She ran up to me, hugged and kissed me. She started talking so fast, telling me about all the shit she had been going through. And how happy she was that I was home. She said, "now that you home, I know I ain't got to worry about going through that bullshit no more." The issue was with the so-called pimps trying to force Candy to hoe for them, the old hoe's not wanting Candy on the strip because once the tricks saw Candy they didn't want them old ass hoes.

It was always females crazy about me. I never tried to figure out why. Yeah, I was always bold, but never whoreish. If I liked a girl alot I would approach her ass and straight up, asking for the pussy. Females talk, especially in the projects. I had females tell me what they liked about me. A lot of females thought that I was cute. Some liked my style. The way I walked, talked and dressed. Some even liked that I was crazy. Some wanted to see if it was true what they heard about how a nigga fucked. I just used to laugh at they asses. I didn't care for the fast girls like that. Tina had become my woman. She was 100% down for me too. Once she revealed that she had this dude that would give her money to a sugar daddy, that put her in the same category as Candy withme. Tina just wasn't on the streets, but she would still turn a trick. That shit turned me off on Tina since I never desired to be a pimp. I loved too hard as a young nigga to pimp. But I do love me a hoe because at least you know she's a hoe! Sounds confusing? I was raised in confusion, so yeah it's confusing! I love me a hoe' although I can't stand the hoe that's in the hoe. One thing for sho,' I do know that she is a hoe! If one can handle the hoe in a woman she is totally loyal to you as your woman.

Most men don't understand the true nature of a woman. There is nothing that can destroy a woman. Now real shit, a man can be destroyed by a woman! A woman is resilient. She can bounce back from anything. There is nothing that can destroy a woman. Some good dick might distract her for a minute, but that's only for the moment. Don't get too comfortable nigga. A woman is going to leave that ass if you're on that dumb shit and she really be loving yo' ass. Bye Bye, nigga. Real shit. Seriously, just think of all the shit a woman manages on a day-to-day basis. Everybody depends on her for damn near everything every day. A woman will work 2 jobs, while going to school, take care of 2 or 3 kids all by herself and still hold a nigga down on lock down. That's real shit! A woman is always a man's most valuable asset. Take care of that woman nigga and she will most certainly take care of you!

Another muthafuckin' crossroad

Once I went back out south, the criminal shit started to happen. I would be introduced to a lick and turned my brothers on to it. I wasn't into breaking into shit like the warehouse of hair products. The Carefree Curl Kits. Activator. Conditioner. And Moisturizer hair spray. A partner of mine had already broken in the place. I just happened to have run into him, after the fact. He couldn't get much shit because he was on bike. I drove him to the place, we filled up the car, and left the warehouse door unlocked. I put Kenny Wayne, Fudd, and Ronald Newsome up on it. We cleaned the place out. Flooded University Court, with hair products. But the real shit, I sold to my Uncle Bally. It was everything needed to supply a beauty shop, with a year of supplies, and he bought it all. I believe someone in the family started a beauty shop or opened one with all that shit.

Both were sent to prison for that shit. Fudd did about 9 months and got out. Kenny Wayne, about 3 years. It ended up being good for Kenny Wayne ass, he got out in 85-86 and ain't ever been back. Congrats Nigga, you did good! That was 36 years ago. Today is, April 5, 2022 and I am at a Maximum-Security Correctional Center awaiting the decision of the Board of Paroles. After that shit with Kenny Wayne and Fudd, I called myself chillin'. But shit was getting crazier and crazier every day.

What'cha Expect Nigga

Alfonzo Burns, was once my nigga. We weren't kickin' it as we once did because of him putting his hands on my cousin Sabrina. The real kill or be killed shit between him and I started because he hit my cousin Sabrina in the mouth with a pair of handlebars. It knocked all of her front teeth out. I had run into Sabrina, she was running in my direction with her hands held over her mouth. I took my hands and moved her hands from her mouth. I asked her, "what happened to you?" She said, "Fonzo." I was in search of him, when he noticed me. He broke low and I started bustin'. He had a distance on me, and I was knockin' chunks out tha' projects bricks try'na hit his ass! Ms. Dorthy tried to talk to me, and I respected Ms. Dorthy, but at that moment I had no comprehension of understanding nothing other than me killin' that nigga. I told Ms. Dorthy, "I'm sorry, but if I catch him, I'm gone kill 'em." I meant that! I expected him to be on the gangsta shit too. Remember he was once my nigga, but I was on some real killa nigga type shit and he wasn't. I got a visit from an old gangsta nigga. A gangsta nigga, well known by many other gangsta niggas. Pool stick pulled up on me. He said, "Nephew come here. That shit with Fonzo, y'all kill that shit. We family. Turned out, Alfonzo was his nephew. And that killed that shit, instantly. But more shit kept popping up. I had to pistol whip a pimp about Candy. This nigga had Candy tied spread eagle, face down on the bed, and had been beating her with a clothes hanger. A clothes hanger was supposed to be the hoe breaker. There ain't many bitches that can stand up to that clothes hanger. He was trying to make her submit to him as her pimp. One of his hoes ran into me on the pike, put me up on what was going on, and took me to the bottom where Candy was at. Once I saw Candy, I snapped. Beat that nigga with the pistol. Fucked him up! Made the hoes untie Candy and help her get dressed. I took all the niggas money and jewelry. One of his hoes had a car. It was four hoes who left with us. The bitch that was driving went to hotel 21 on Murfreesboro Road and got 2 rooms. I stayed with them hoe's for about 10 days, until Candy got better. The hoes wanted me to be they pimp. I had a stable of professional hoes who had chosen up on me and I turned them down. I wasn't no pimp. I was a gangsta.

I have a saying, mind over matter: if you don't mind, it don't muthafuckin' matter. That hoe and pimp shit is mind over matter shit for me. I do muthafuckin' mind, and it do muthafuckin' matter! I don't want no female that suck dick and fuck for a living. I can't relax and enjoy you. Kiss and caress you and do no type of passionate nothing with you. My dick ain't tender, but my heart is. I believe in love. But, once a woman be unfaithful to me, she gets no more respect. I believe in true love. I know that being unfaithful ain't true love. When a woman cheat on me she becomes a bitch and a hoe. I become a nigga and a pimp! You dirty bitch. Come on hoe let's do this pimp and hoe' shit!

Love Changes

One day Candy said to me, "you don't love me no moe cause if you did you would kick my ass for the shit I be doing. I be doing shit so you will kick my ass for doing it and let me know that you still care about me." Candy understood that a man that loved her would have been correcting her for her bullshit. It's the reality of crazy love when you're living a crazy life. Candy was hurt that I had stopped caring about whatever she did. I had fallen out of love with Candy, she was right. I had love for her, but I had lost my passion and desire. I still would shoot a nigga or bitch for fuckin' with Candy because she was a part of me, but my love for her had changed. In love's reality, no man can pimp a woman that he truly loves. If a woman truly loves a man, she is not going to lay down with another man. THE TRUTH! Therefore, to be a pimp you got to be heartless. To be a hoe, you got to be heartless. Two heartless muthafuckas make the perfect muthafuckin' couple. THE TRUTH!

Knowledge And Wisdom

It was a struggle to love Candy because I couldn't love her completely. At our age, during that time, we were supposed to have been just having fun. Fucking a lot and being happy with us just being in love. Due to me dealing with Candy, it was not a mother in University Court that wanted me dealing with their daughters. How could I blame them? That added to my anger. Although I had a few older women that I was able to fuck, I wanted a fresh young sister that was 16 or 17, no kids, and who hadn't already been fucked by 10 different niggas at 16 or 17 years of age.

What got me hooked on Candy was she needed me. She captured that side of me that needed to be needed. That is a natural element of a need built inside of all of us. It is more than a desire. It is a need. We are inspired and motivated, out of our need, to be needed. It gives us strength. It gives more meaning to life. However, in love it is more precious to be wanted more than needed. I never had a high school sweetheart. Hell, I never completed high school. Nothing about how I came up was normal. Yet, from where I came up it was the norm.

The Beginning of the end

At 18 years old, I am freshly released from Taft Youth Center. I had no value for life, not my life, so surely not the life of another muthafucka'. I was angry! Filled with hurt, disappointment, and unhappiness. I was raised in a household of nothing but drama. A real muthafuckin' environment of against all odds. Not that we didn't have things, the environment was mentally, physically, emotionally, and spiritually unhealthy. Period! It took its toll on me. I became one of the worst types that the environment creates. To me, my hood was a killing field. I was ready to introduce you to it! That simple.

Although I came up in what to me is a real devil's den, to us it's love in tha' hood. We weren't exposed to the evils of racism in the hood like it is in everyday life in America for blacks. We live in our own world in the hood. Really not feeling the deepness of the hatred that White America felt toward us. I can say that because as a child I wasn't taught about the race shit. People didn't explain it. When I was going to school, out south, all our teachers were black. They taught us. It wasn't until we moved to East Nashville, that I was exposed to whites and started to see and feel the energy of racism. I learned fast that they didn't want me at their schools. The white teachers showed favoritism toward the white kids. In turn, the white kids were bold with, white privilege. What they didn't know is they were dealing with a different generation of niggas. We didn't have that turn the other check mentality. We had that fuck you, you white muthafuckin' muthafucka' if you call me a nigga, I'm gon' kick yo' white ass. Many of them was bold enough to try it, and they got they ass kicked. My generation were the fuck the white folks generation! We rejected their schools, their jobs, and their law. We beat them up, fucked they daughters, robbed, and stole from they ass. We rejected white America and created a new way of being and doing things as blacks in America!

Fuck It All

I came up so fast, most people thought that I was just as old as my big brother Fudd. I was a muthafucka', if must say so myself. I mixed in with all the crazy shit. As I said before, I started all the dice games in the "Ramaz." I was in the middle of the war between Dee

Dee and Tony Smith. They were partners at one time, and they both were like big brothers to me. I don't know what they fell out about. I just remember Dee Dee, and I was standing beside his car and Tony Smith pops up from out of nowhere taking shit to Dee Dee.

He said, " I got'cha ass. I told'gha I was gon'get'cha nigga. You must've thought I was playing. It's still yo lucky day. Cause at first, I was gon kill ya'. But, since we were partners for so long I ain't gon kill ya but I gotta shoot'cha. So which leg do you want it in, the right or the left one?"

"Tony, you can't shoot Dee Dee." I jumped in front of Dee Dee.

Tony told me, "get out of the way lil bruh."

Then Dee Dee, caught Tony slippin'. And I repeated the same shit, jumping in front of Tony. Except, Tony pushed me out of the way. He said to Dee Dee, "now you know if you shoot me and don't kill me what it's gon' be. I could've killed you the other day, but I didn't because of lil bruh" as he pointed to me. Tony Smith was a killa, for real! He had already killed two niggas, since he had come back from Vietnam. Dee Dee was a rider. More of a criminal mind, but he would kill if need be.

I was able to stop them niggas from killing each other. They both loved me, and it was only because of me that one of them didn't die at the hands of the other. With Dee Dee, it was always some crazy shit. We was always in some shit. With Tony, he wasn't on the same shit. All the niggas in Rock City families had a lil money. All of them niggas came up in a strong family structure. Pasha. Ronald Newsome. Dee Dee, and Tony. All their parents were married and had been together forever. They all graduated from school. And it was always smooth. Especially Pasha.

Auntie Pam

Auntie Pam had come to get me and Candy from out South. She was trying to get me out of the streets after hearing about me shooting people and shit. Plus, she wanted to show me how to make real money with Candy. Auntie had rich white men flying in from Texas who were seriously interested in young girls like Candy. We go to auntie house and as we walked through the door, Candy was offered $200. Still, the whole time I was there I was thinking about them projects. I really didn't care about anything going on in that house. I was in a hurry to get to that crazy shit going on the hood, the loud music, and people out running around all night. All the crazy shit that I hated so much, yet loved at the same damn time. I had started to become what I hated so much.

Back to the killing fields

University muthafuckin' Court. Nigga, welcome to the Killin' Fields. As I moved back out there, my dangerous level went up 10 notches. My whole mentality went to zero understanding. I became a trigger-happy ass nigga. I was shooting nigga for the smallest shit. I was all the way gone. I mean ALL THE WAY GONE! Young dudes who were my age, but not on that gun shit. Niggas approaching me about they girlfriend, an ass I grabbed. Yeah, I was wrong for grabbing her ass, but still nigga what? Dumb ass young nigga, approaching me ready to fight and end up getting shot. Not in the leg. In the face, chest or stomach.

I didn't see a future for me. Mentally I was already destroyed. I was a man without a dream, with no sense of direction. My life had no value to me. Everything that I was taught that I was supposed to love hadn't done nothing but hurt me. Fuck the shit going on in white America, I was living in a muthafuckin' war zone in the house where I had to sleep every night. The shit that the white folks did to me wasn't shit compared to the shit my brother was doing to me. He is the real cause behind how violent I had become. Anybody that I shot, stabbed or beat with a brick, stick, bat or whatever was catching the built-up shit that I wanted to do to my brother. For many years I seriously wanted to kill my brother.

One day I was going to stab his ass in his sleep. He had hit me in my face in my sleep. Moms knew that we had been fighting earlier and she heard me in the kitchen going through her knives. I got the sharpest one. I eased into the room where he was asleep. I came up with the knife, and as I did, I heard my mother say, "don't do it, please don't do it." Kenny Wayne woke up and I told him, "You lucky cause I was getting ready to kill you." For all the years I spent in prison I felt like I suppose to have been there for killing my brother. I didn't really want to share this part of my story. But it's a major part of my life that helped to create the violent person that I became. A sad part of my reality.

My brother and I's relationship will never be as close as it could have been, but it surely isn't as bad as it used to be. We all must learn how to let go of yesterdays pains to truly enjoy the pleasures of tomorrow's joys, my new reality.

You can't save us, if we don't wanna be saved

I had so many trying to save me. Auntie Pam. Uncle Bally. Auntie LuLu. Gran-momma, Queen Violet Rose Corley. Uncle Tick. Auntie May'ran. Auntie Jackie. My mother. I was too caught up in a I-don't-give-a-fuck mentality, and I got I-don't-give-a-fuck results.

Auntie Cheryl tried to give Candy stability in a healthy family structured environment and all her girls accepted Candy, like a sister. Reka, Meka, Nikita and Brea, but Candy couldn't adapt to the normality of a happy family structured environment. She was already trapped in the lifestyle of being a hoe and deep inside I think she loved it.

Candy was on my ass about pimpin'. The hoes wanted to be identified as my hoes to help keep them gorilla pimps up off they ass. Everybody that knew anything about me knew without a doubt that I was "retarded" with or without that pistol. I was totally committed to the gangsta shit. I wasn't no robber. That shit started as a spring off from the racist shit that a nigga went through in East Nashville. As I said earlier, it wasn't until we moved to the "Ramaz" that I learned how whites felt about us. They were openly bold about it. That teacher called me a nigga, that's why I smacked that bitch. Second time my mother had told me that I was lucky that they didn't kill me. Especially with me smacking a white woman. Still, I didn't give a fuck. I would've smacked that bitch again, if she called me a nigga again.

Remember I was speaking about me riding the short bus. Well, after being embarrassed about riding the bus one time, I made the driver let me off at the bottom of Straightway. I'm walking up Straightway, and I heard, " nigga." Pow, I'm hit in the head with something. I grab my head; my head is wet. It's dark red blood on my hand. Every time a car would drive by, I would jump in the bushes. That shit seriously affected me, I was in fear. It changed something deep inside of me. Once I was back out South, the anger released itself against all whites who had the misfortune of crossing my path. I would just beat the whites until they were seriously fucked up. I wouldn't take their money at first. Robbery was never the motive. My reason was strictly to beat they ass to damn near death! One day, I caught this white dude in JC. He was selling household shit like pots and pans and shit. I just pistol whipped his ass and left his ass fucked up. The young niggaz that watched me beat that white muthafucka' went in his pockets, took his money, ran me down and gave me some of it. From that day forward I started robbing they ass too. That's the shit I was on when Terry and WC started running with me.

Shit that just happens

WC, Terry and I had been hanging together for about a week when UNC, Terry, and I was walking to the liquor store when this tall ass punk said, "look at them 3 phine muthafucka's right there."

Unc asked, "who you talking too?"

The punk said, "all three of you phine ass niggas!

"Give me your gun nephew."

He called himself going to pistol whip the punk. But, when he came up with the pistol to hit the punk, he had to jump because the punk was so tall. He hit the punk with tha' pistol. The punk caught Unc in the air and smacked Unc too. Unc went one way, the pistol went the other; we all went for the pistol. I came up with it and shot tha' punk. I had too, the punk was trying to still grab tha' gun. After I shot him Unc got the gun back and stood over the punk. The punk begged Unc, "please don't kill me. Please. Please don't kill me. I'm sorry." Unc said something crazy to the punk. We went on to the liquor store like nothing ever happened. We came right back the same way, 10 minutes later.

Niggas Play Too Damn Much And Shit Be Real, For Real!

A few days later, I woke up about 12 noon. I'm heading to the store to get me a black label beer. My brother Jr. stopped and asked if I had a joint. I didn't have one, I had 7 dollars, so, I gave him 5, to get a sack with and told him to meet me back at the house. He got my last five dollars and kept going with it. I was mad as hell all day. I ran into him around 8 that night, at the liquor store. He was in the car with Boy Baby, RIP, and Shawn Elam. I approached the car to get my money from my brother. He decides he wanna show out and gets to talking crazy. Before I could even stop myself, I came up with tha' gun and shot inside the car. The bullet hit Shawn in the face. I still regret that shit til this very day. Shawn, bruh I apologize. From my heart man, I apologize!

After that shit I just really went crazy. I was robbing and beating every white muthafucka I had the chance to get. Unc got caught up in a robbery that we did, but he was the only one identified. He was already on paper, so he couldn't make a bond.

Fudd got paroled on that burglary, so he wasn't hanging with us during the time that I had really snapped out. Fonzo, had already taken a warrant out on me for shooting at him. I thought it was gangsta between us. I was already wanted. I was a suspect in 3 or 4 other shootings, plus a suspect in two other murders that I knew nothing whatsoever about. Shit was just hitting a nigga all at once.

Auntie May'ran, was still in the house at 109 Wharf Ave. Her 2 kids, Darryl and Denise, were there with her and the lights in the house were out. I was on the prawl to get the money to get the lights on, when I ran across this white dude at the liquor store cashing a check for about $1200. I immediately zoomed in on him. He came up out of the store walking toward the bottom, with this black girl. I started walking in the same direction. The white dude kept looking back at me, so I said something to him. He responded with some smart shit like "why you following me?" I said, "Nigga, I ain't following you. You just walking in the same direction I'm walking." He said something else smart. I snapped on his ass, I came up with tha' pistol and robbed his ass. I gave them the money to get the lights on. It couldn't be paid until the next day. I got drunk and ran around in the projects most of the night, by myself. I was tired from the last few weeks that I had been running crazy doing way too much. It was about 1:30 a.m. and I was tired as hell.

People in UC were avoiding me because of all the shooting I had done. Plus, you know how gossip spreads especially in the projects. It was being said that I had killed somebody. I could feel that something wasn't right. I was so tired I wasn't paying close enough attention. I saw the police creeping through the projects, rolling' slowly. What I didn't know was that it was me who they were watching. I noticed two 2 police cars parked on Wharf Ave, right down the street from the house. Still, I went straight in the house, laid on the floor, and fell asleep. I awake to muthafucka's screaming something. I was reaching for my gun, when I heard, "don't move! Put your hands where I can see them." It was the muthafuckin' police.

To Be Continued!

Made in the USA
Columbia, SC
02 October 2024